Eléna Rivera was born in Mexico City and raised in Paris. Her most recent book is *Scaffolding* (Princeton University Press, 2017). Her book *The Perforated Map* was published by Shearsman in 2011. She received a National Endowment for the Arts in translation (2010) received the Robert Fagles Translation Prize (2011) and fellowships from Trelex Paris Poetry Residency (2019) and MacDowell (2020).

Also by Eléna Rivera

Scaffolding, Princeton Series of Contemporary Poets, Princeton University Press, Princeton, NJ
Light Tremor, Estepa Editions, Artist Book, Kate van Houton, Paris
Le Souci Formel/The Formal Concern, Chaplet #211, Belladonna, Brooklyn, NY
Disturbances in an Ocean of Air (French/English, translated by the author), Artist Book, concept and lithography, Kate van Houton, Estepa Editions, Paris
The Perforated Map, Shearsman Books, Bristol
A Test of Labor, in *Labor Poetic Labor! 2: into the archive, essaypress.o*rg, Athens, OH
Atmosphered, Oystercatcher Press, Cambridge
Overture, http://www.metambesen.org/books, Annandale-on-Hudson, NY
On the Nature of Position and Tone, Fields Press, Chicago, IL & New York, NY
Remembrance of Things Plastic, LRL e- editions, San Marcos, TX
In Respect of Distance, Beard of Bees #45, Chicago, IL
Mistakes, Accidents and a Want of Liberty, Barque Press, Cambridge
Disturbances in An Ocean of Air, Phylum Press, Hamden, CT
Suggestions at Every Turn, Seeing Eye Books, Los Angeles, CA
Unknowne Land, Kelsey Street Press, Berkeley, CA
Wale, or The Corse, Leave Books, Buffalo, NY

Translations

Body Was by Isabelle Garron, Litmus Press, Brooklyn, NY (forthcoming)
The Ink's Path by Bernard Noël, Les éditions Cadastre8zéro, artwork by François Rouan, Paris
The Rest of the Voyage by Bernard Noël, Graywolf Press, St. Paul, MN
Parting Movement, Constantly Prevented, Isabelle Baladine Howald, Oystercatcher Press
The Pain of Returning, by Isabelle Baladine Howald, Mindmade Books, Los Angeles, CA
Secret of Breath by Isabelle Baladine Howald, Burning Deck Press, Providence, RI

Eléna Rivera

Epic Series

Shearsman Books

First published in the United Kingdom in 2020 by
Shearsman Books Ltd
PO Box 4239
Swindon
SN3 9FN

Shearsman Books Ltd Registered Office
30–31 St. James Place, Mangotsfield, Bristol BS16 9JB
(this address not for correspondence)

www.shearsman.com

ISBN 978-1-84861-732-2

Copyright © Eléna Rivera, 2020.
The right of Eléna Rivera to be identified as the author
of this work has been asserted by her in accordance with the
Copyrights, Designs and Patents Act of 1988.
All rights reserved.

Acknowledgments

My gratitude and thanks to the following editors/publishers where earlier versions of these poems were first published: Kristin Prevallet, Juliana Spahr and Mark Wallace, et. al. for publishing *Wale; or The Corse*, Leave Books; Kathleen Fraser for selecting *Unknowne Land* for the Frances Jaffer book award published by Patricia Dienstfrey and Rena Rosenwasser of Kelsey St. Press; and to Dale Going who published an early variant of *The Wait; for Homer's Penelope*, EM Press.

My admiration and gratitude to Carol Snow for her feedback and comments on the manuscript and whose friendship has been indispensable. I also wish to thank Denise Newman, Russell Switzer, Myung Mi Kim, Denise Liddell Lawson, Thom Donovan, Anne Carson, Kathleen Hill, Alison Bundy, Joan Retallack, and Gabrielle Civil for their support and art which has buoyed me over the years.

My appreciation and thanks to Tony Frazer, indefatigable publisher, for his generous work on behalf of this book, and for all he has done and is doing for poetry.

And finally many thanks to Rebab El Sadek for her artwork and Scott David Gordon for the use of his photograph for the cover of this book.

Contents

Wale; or The Corse / 7

Unknowne Land / 37
Fire / 41
Earth / 49
Water / 61
Air / 71
The Sphere / 81

The Wait; for Homer's Penelope / 95

Notes / 137

I went out in the woods. Instead
was mentioned, an action
revived. Going into the unknown
with which I am fully familiar
You remember the seeds? …

                John Cage

when you become attuned to your attunement
to scarring, then you're on your way

                Fred Moten

WALE;

or

The Corse

"Open your lips; don't open them simply.
I don't open them simply."

A book might spill out, desperate, moody
savage, spouting off white characters,
until death do us part. She cannot open her
lips simply because it would be heroism.
The words caught in her throat and the out
pour when and if it came would leave a
pale and turbid wake.

(A toad stuck on scotch tape.)

She drinks water. Open so that she may
enter. She wanted to step into a world
of walruses and whales, but the war stopped
any further plans from forming. She asks you
to take care of the gift of her abandonment.

Alone at her table, lips pressed together,
the writing shuts us out and brings her in.
She asks us to be a dream which cracks open.

I

knots

knew it

came

critiqued

I

starved

in one place

wore the same

thought that

woeful way

lost

"Whole world seems against me if I could
just explain. Man I love has left me because
I called…"

Dust on the window. Blue light catches
the red of the lamp (turned off). She claims

her ring another time. Woe. Woe. Woe. Woe.
Woe. Woe. Woe. This man interested her

at once. Translating all things to numbers,
the cat waved. He came over after playing

the set and asked, are you in my distance?
Did the man know that the call caused

bombs to drop into another child's backyard?
He took delight in departure.

driven

smoke moved

crated

different

grew in many

an ignorant whim

to please

She gives deeper joy, consumes more swiftly.

She eats as though she was starving. Hair
in place. Her mother associated all that was
ugly with what was hateful. She hated her
stomach (which "She" do you mean?). She sat
in the corner where we put her, facing a wall.
Your friendship was her sorrow. Pain went
both ways. The stolen, stolen was the measure
of grief. Her house was bombed in half. Had
to run. Had to run. Had to run. In half a
person cannot be. Not fully be. No fill.
She asked if she could eat more. (Again
which "She" do you mean? Make yourself
clear.) She said yes—sausages, eggs, toast.
Disgust. The Rise was reflected in all these
eyes that stared. Took sides for survival.
The glass is empty and being filled was
never understood. SATIATED. The woman
dressed in tattoos said that word, said there
was nothing like it. She held the girl in her arms.
You can't white that out.

a whole

occupied

I watched

a travesty

trea

ted

To be furious is to be frightened out
of fear.

How many more until we begin
mourning? She bleeds into her Thai food,
into…. Her breasts swell slightly.

They were associated by color; a paper
clip holds them together. The air weighs,
weighs heavily, and whether it is reality
or not, she can never entirely settle.

We insisted on a gate. How could she?
Leaves were pressed in a thick book, and
later she drew them with children.

The sun shines in at the window and
women were open (soft skin easily bruises).
How much longer will her father continue
to shake her? She can't listen to doors
slam. Slam!

The bar was crowded, cramped. People in
leather jackets. The man never returned the
ring the woman lost (though they laid down,
laid down—not standing, as to kill time—
and he hurt her). Fortunately pain lasts only
a short time and Civilization is what was best
and most suitable for all.

out

side

pressed

worry molded

pain

I

late

lament

"Her cry silences whole vocabularies of
names for things."

There is no access when the destruction
is so great. Only leisure will bring you
towards the knowledge of who you are.
The shade is half open, just enough to brighten
the room so as to not need a lamp. Craving
will manifest itself in arranging and rearranging
(enters ghost). You did this to your children.
She does this to her compositions. Will you be
her audience if she promises to be soft
enough, smell good enough, curve her body
into yours enough? The woman "sold her soul"
for attention (she must resign her life into the
hands of he who steers the boat). A mouse is
ineffective, especially when still. Strum your
guitar and you'll hear in it an echo (with hands
that steer). Perhaps, she wets her hair so that it
will bounce back.

tape

book

letter

candle

wail

pen

log

saliva

sheet

radio

knife

The woods chopped down describe
seduction to the lonely.

The audience which we are becomes
that leaf and then falls into waterfalls
(or something else) flakes off down
the highway.

A pregnant lesson in solemn tones.
The continual tolling of a bell in a ship
that is foundering at sea in a fog.

She is still (still, still, still)
and puts herself into seclusion.

aim at

tender

timber

Fall into

gallows

tight

"I am tormented with an everlasting itch
for things remote."

She struggles with the scales on his back,
licks the betrothal clean. Water in a long
stemmed glass beckons the plunge, perhaps
a projectile. She searches for a vision in his
eyes though he turns away. Magpies stop
the penetration. He only goes half-way then
decides he doesn't like his part in the last act.
She slides down to the bear who would
be her mate (tiddely pom). Across oceans
the situation shows its face as performing
(calling itself) nicely.

in

a

falling train

I

trail

towards

the street

Curious sight

"Meditation and water are wedded forever."

    She shies away from your scrutiny. Bring
her our treasures beneath the ocean and unveil

    your secrets, but do not take away from
her the combustion. Seduction is best left at

    the entrance (or would it be simpler if
she used different words?) She will be able to

    speak (inside an/other). Expansion through
the foundation of Americans still fighting. She

    desires your shift. A move towards an
unremembered chair. Simple on the surface but

    beneath? Simple on the surface (she wrote
the history) and the difference was perceived

    with downcast eyes. Nothing will come of
(simple on the surface) Nothing will come of

where are

the charts

drawn

up

for this

relation

in transit

how will it

The sky isn't up there; it's between us.

She expands into whiteness, not knowing
how to touch you. It is her history. She
knows that green leaves are also a part of
it. What color a country is really depends
on the map. Who chose orange for Russia?
The color of Lear's shadow? She feels water
fill her as she expands. Round stomach.
Would you take her part? (Moves center stage.)
Dignity is difficult in sandals and the
dictionary only turns with the help of her
hand (having left the chapel before the
benediction). She turns away, hears but
doesn't listen to a language remote (moan).
They were but butterflies and died. She
pierces and cracks and colors. They were
her heroes and fell.

fast

funeral

no

time

for the

fiddler

to steer

and form

our finest

The plot has thickened, a twist of fate
reverberates, seals their death.

After three years housekeeping on the wide
ocean, the sun-lit room was now wrapped
in darkness. The bed sealed with stitches loosens
though it likes to be private when sleeping.

A good laugh is a good thing and the story
could have been a virtuous one but she inter
rupted it by reading *Hamlet* for the second time.
What is it but to make thy sepulcher and creep
into it far before thy time. A full stomach
weighs heavy upon the spine who breathes the
energy meant to continue, continue. Rest not
upon my soul, thou might discoverest that thou
art dead. Ahhh… (pause) Ahhh… (pause) It
can't be possible. Oh man, oh man (turns towards
the audience), that is her tale in three acts.

Good night pious folks, a mild voice said with
unassuming authority and ordered the scattered
people to condense, the machine will rebroadcast this
violence tomorrow.

distort

the bend

in the house

plant which

grew unreasonable

when I went out

of town for a swim

more and more unfolding its noiseless
and measureless leaves

She pretends and inside, a hollow ring —
strikes paralyzing, strikes dumb, strikes the
senses numb. A smile will not satisfy a heart
which is distanced by onslaughts of Northern
winds. Try to ring a bell while trumpets
blow. The big band plays over loudspeakers
as the world and its details pass. She admits
the rage and hatred in her heart to no one,
not even herself (this is a dream) refusing
to be comforted. She walks down city streets,
a yellow light (pause). Should you ever be
athirst in the great America the fire hydrant
will only extinguish street fires. The silent storm
though won't reach inside walls to drown
out all thought, all delusion. The woman bends
over and feels the folds weigh heavy on her.

the grief

bent

in a small

scalp-knot

was not

felt by

fingers

in my hair

A loud animal sob, like that of a moose.

She saw a stripe in the wide blue sky.

Bridge the gap with suns and moons, or
cover it over with an essence of whiteness.

Her heart will not be quiet, quiet girl.
She said she longed for some awakening
through memory but no one understood.

Who would understand a closed book and
looking at its size, give up that sail
and stare out of spotted windows.

She watched the trees bend in the Pacific
wind (trees in the background sway).

She asked, and wondered why she felt, the
language the man had written as her own,
as the rhythm of timed lights.

She opens to the Pirate who caught her.

coming

back

already

com

ing

back

plunged

into

the

mute

bir

th

I

In narrative writing, always indicate the transition
from the general to the particular.

The next morning, breakfast. She gets out
of the shoe. He makes love to her. She wakes
her laugh, separately. Silence pushes down
as she keeps rising to put away pots and pans.
The white smell plays the violin as she picks
at her fingernails, touches her lips. At the
entrance a birthday cake is interrupted. She
gets sick again, hated to share. Her lips
pressing themselves together felt the beat
through wood floors and cement walls. Change
from one form, state, subject, place, to the
specific. Her nose had an itch and she desired
to touch it. Moved to the other room, the
dining room. Ah and has fingers; they all move,
but not all together. There ARE differences.
She now prophesies that she will dismember her
dismemberer. A few were left behind, that is
what happens to children. Generally though
ice cream or cake or candy is used.

the flight

froze

be

sides

fuchsias

dead

in the water

"The whale cannot digest me."

A step into unknown territory, exploring space between skins.

She heard the voice from the other room, remembering familiar ache, familiar house.

Please play, she asked, not knowing to ask for what she needed. Only able to lie beneath the heat and be penetrated. There were steps taken, for everyone knows this earthly air is terribly infected with the nameless miseries of those who died exhaling it.

I

rise

ridge

glide

re

dry

She

swam

one

place

you

read

UNKNOWNE LAND

the sound of the land—erupts—recite after me—a route—a river road—saturated—leads to the next, and the next—shatters and uncovers—recite after me—a memory, a reflection, a word, a meadow—where are the lost—charred—I drift amidst—*and the earth was filled with*

FIRE

Who bears a record of the world?

Exploding.   At the beginning   there

were no witnesses, and now   we are under

the weight of illumination.

Glowing embers
yield up so much.

The figure leans forward.
I am that figure, elbow
down on the desk, full
of North wind; a figure
shown, shorn, fastened
to too many voices.

a burnt child dreads the fire

Behind the framework
a body retreats   and then
again   catapulted forward—
into a lament, pulled into
the rhythm of the pencil
as it adheres to the page,
in the quivering cold wind,
fastening the flame to the glass.

Find the right word,
stripped bare of its berries.

A small body is bent over a large
white sheet of paper. She draws.
She draws what pleases her. She
does not calculate her seclusion,
does not choose or think how the
drawing will come out beforehand.

nocturnal winds down an alley

I look for her who was chiseled.
I am lifted from one meaning
to the next—bent over. I do not
find. I am chosen. I make
the trip into distance, the path
that separates two points.

What to do with a red child,
scribbled on a piece of paper?

In the interval, between childhood
and when the figure was clothed.
The moment midway (putting
on the bra), halfway (pulling up
the underwear), between being nude
then clothed. A private space
set burning. Closed and nude.

where there is much light
the shadows are deepest

Between what you need
and what she needs   (intense,
turbulent, furious, destructive).
I step into the room. I am stepping
into, step in. Ruins at the border.
I follow the glimpse, the "almost."

Scarlet, rubiate, sanguine, carmine.
Not as honest with myself as I

Simulate a tale, a way out
of the cinders (where she was
headed), full of expectations,
in her superimposed box.
She puts on her uniform,
white shirt, gray skirt,
dark blue pullover.

a torn limb held out toward the sun

She speaks in another language.
I confused her movements with
the space around her. I tried to
follow her, an intervention of the
alternate line; I tried to live her
secrets, her fantasy, even though
it came hard (hearing).

Created! Gleaming! Glowing!
The liberating scream that sticks in your throat.

Captive. She finds her notes
are connected by a bind. She
hovers over the debris. Cut and
fastened in a conch—confined
to the limits given (not her own)
a piece of (through a grid)
W. . . W. . . Wo. . .

a wide open mouth with no sound

She is gone—
Spread wide for idolaters:
Daughter of   'man'
sculptured, taken, chosen. Am I
suitably shaped to generate?
(*the sound of the land*) to create?
(*the sound*) Where can I find her?

EARTH

Behold Now, The Ground Beneath,

brings only   to the eyes of those

who   traveled   across   it

far   and   wide.

"Nothing will be retained from them

which they have imagined to do."

Le premier mot	take the field	*Le premier bruit*
hold still	*Quelle est la forme?*	hold the needle still
Quelle est la ligne?	make the mark	*Quelle est la phrase?*
even more painterly	*A la recherche d'un mot*	enter the hole
Cette contradiction	in a composition	*Le premier mot*
lines converge	*Le précipice?*	that very point

At the epigean divisions along racial, sexual, moralistic and intellectual lines   a forest of factories   so that whatever side we're on we stand stagnating   *Any little bit will do to pull the rest through*   this clogged surface   *slide right in* this cavity filled with noise   (exfoliated)   this lattice of words   *Tellement fragile*   this agitated landscape (built by accretion)   this opening at the top *Quel est le mot*   that had once been so beautiful

We (the family group) were scattered abroad more than once (a familiar labyrinth)   so we moved closer together (the padlock fastened so that one couldn't breathe)   In the bowels of the telluric, between highways and the steady march of time, we remained motionless   we hid from the nightmare (A book in which only certain chapters are read, others ignored) How else can one live on the soft wet earth?   plotting objects in a packed room   "—Do not our lives consist of the four elements?"   *Intruding on some intimacy*   "—Faith, so they say, but I think it rather consists of eating and drinking." At the crossroads a counterpart is sung: One   the diaphragm expands   Two   *Now is the hour*   Three for the mouth   Four   to   open
Some   things   have   to   be   repeated

The soil around these grounds must first be tested before one can begin building   (so the pieces will fit together in the end)   Soil, in a period of physiologically enforced dormancy, cannot produce brooks of water, fountains that spring out from valleys and hills, land that produces wheat and barley   The vine, the fig tree, the pomegranate were frozen in a ditch   Olives and honey trampled in an open field   The murmur of Arctic winds a reminder of what had to be dug up   Our testimony Our walled in tragedy   Our new dwelling, expelled from space and time   (soil being a living organism ready to adapt and change at a moment's notice) Our   clouded   space   expands   and   contracts All parts are related to the whole   Look: A word can be insuperable   Another, a tabernacle

One can be so careful that one can become a mere ghost   *Hunters are in the forest go in and wear red* or a handful of bones   *Devils are in the desert go in and bear yellow*   The heart is taken out as if it were a splinter, in one sweeping gesture   Our terrain trembled, trampled by so many boots: left, left, left right left   "the noises in the darkness of the night"   left, left, left right left   "the groans of the wounded"   left, left, left right left   "filled with their cries"   left, left, left right left   What happened once we left the cell though   is another story (the other side of the window)   a book that tells the secret about life in North America   which coast are you willing to enter? Embedded in rock   One person's struggle illuminates the rest Light kept trying to force itself in   *Hide in another name* though I was practically blindfolded   *Hide deep inside*

A landscape can be viewed from any window   "An altar of stone" frames the opening through which we see   (and moving it no easy business)   its weight casts an anchor in a desert   (sand or snow) or a jungle   (city or Amazonian)   "Brought forth into this wilderness"   what is seen confined to what one wants to see (some towers have no windows)   or the discovery sighted limited to our particular imagination   We put a yoke around it and demanded that it should serve us   no questions asked Hardened and held in servitude   *then pulled back*   while a tough musculature grew around my bowels   What seeds were planted? the knot is tightened   Who made those abusive remarks? sothatIcouldn'tfeel,   respondtomyownflesh,   tothehereandnow? When our house   dangled on a chain   it was not related to the praedial, so we heard the awful screech of metal links

To let the senses roam unfettered, unrestrained by pieces of furniture
But I am immured in this century like a fly in a bog,
a phrase fixated, repeated over and over   This grasping
at spongy ground,   poorly drained,   surrounded by sedges
(A little girl plays a board game)   Looking back at the last pages
(at where she had been)   I taste the salt which falls like pillars
down my cheeks   This touch   This is not what I had in mind
My *faiblesse*   the axis of how I happened
to perceive my earthly existence   *de femme*
Humbled by my predicament   (that of being thrown around,
for example, lifted by his strength and finding myself landed
in the other room)   I decided to grow up (before my time)
until I realized that my project had always been horizontal
"A n   a l i e n   i n   a   s t r a n g e   l a n d"

Who will lie with Him to preserve the seed of the father?
(And this question was asked with perfect seriousness)
To "lie with" involves many kinds of manipulation   (by hand, foot, mouth, lips, penis, or eyes)   and the lover, if predisposed to planting seeds, will walk down long corridors and rot in the soil
Any little bit will do to pull the rest through   "broken me asunder"
The material is measured and cut   "taken me by the neck and"
Sometimes a pattern is used   "shaken me to pieces"
I had to embark remembering   Rationality crawls into the picture, points its finger and gives reasons for the "lying" that was done hundreds of years back   *there are shaded regions*
She shakes bitterly   (light tremble from an outsider's perspective)
each   piece   has   to   be   stitched   together
(earthquakes   were   what   came   to   mind)

In a roomful of people waiting for my marriage, what is generally remembered is that a struggle took place   hesitation confused the current   no clearing   (ask yourself how many of your thoughts are really your own)   a nation grows, sowed, scattered by the dead 'til it no longer has any memory but that which it was given   My feet were firmly planted (I thought) but an unconscious choice was made   surprised by pleasure one can begin to remember that one is not advancing or developing   a "quick" excavation will not give you "the bigger picture"   To observe means to see (a boulder must be removed from the window) things for what they really are   I kept forgetting things, ignoring others   The animal thrown in the cellar   I forgot to keep my senses alert to everything going on around me Until   there   was   nothing   left   but   sounds

I pick up stones one by one: sandstone, obsidian, shale, limestone
"…*all that power sweeping savagely in and inevitably withdrawing, hypnotized, and the two senses of that vastness and this tininess…*"
corundum, carnelian, granite   (It's important not to lose one's notes, or the surface will grow hard and dry like the upper layer of earth around a city)   I look at their shapes: flat, banded, spherulitic, stratified, hexagonal   their textures: smooth, lustrous, sedimentary, crystalline, sharp   *Une pierre*
She finds   places to hide   *Un caillou*
The garden turns to stone until all the shit is washed off
"A word will never be able to comprehend the voice that utters it"

In a body of standing water   *Quel est le mot?*
my companions   as I rested

WATER

Flowing waters,

especially when   bubbling
up from the   interior
of the earth,

are animate and divine.

"I take it slow"
        Sometimes—
                "What if then *is* now?"

Whether flat or sharp
        I follow the notation
                or perhaps I portend

something else—a descent
        in broad daylight,
                from higher to lower,

if you believe in division,
        a desire for something
                more than an heirloom

at the quivering waterline
        More than my hesitation,
                this shudder at the shore

parched with thirst
        on the brink of memory
                at the edge of the surface

Wavering between then
        and now and the rooms that fit
                inside me like columns

Where is the door to this one
        or that one? I watch light
                steal under water

so that it ripples,
        so that snow will melt
                from previously forgotten

silenced or deadened parts
        of the body—the pull of the line,
                as fibers twist and coil

around the corner of my past
        How can I know the present
                if the swollen cry, "Restrain"?

"Excessive!" "Demanding!" "Too…!"
        Those tugs on the leash
                that bled the engram,

that decimated the floorboards,
        that filled the drawer with water
                so that there wouldn't be enough

room remaining, or else flushed
    down the pipes, the impurities
        filtered, and a life force depleted

At the intersection of two
    roads, be not bound by
        cultivation, by exact

measurements; this kind of
    oblivion will cramp and fetter
        the spirit, this "fitting in"

What have we managed to
    change but the surface?
        Nuances. Words used to describe

"Too!" I hear an echo of it
    in my ear, a legacy
        passed on so that I was

split and divided—but I want to
    descend along the dense,
        animate river encircling the earth

I want to glide softly over
    the cold ocean like a Monarch
        butterfly, plunge into its opacity

But I am stopped short—
        gasping, grasping, barely
                a breath in all my…

A mort is heard in the
        distance—a killing is made
                in overwhelming quantities

Minnows balance themselves
        "and the sudden silent trout
                all lit up, hanging,

trembling"   Traveling
        in a felluca through
                a shade called "America"

A past cut in bone
        "What's in a name?"
                A cascade? An ideogram?

An emblem? And beneath it?
        Dominion is devoid of light
                Can't even swim across the moat

I forgot my watercolors
        (flooded with memories of a
                woman and a man fighting over)

The sound of the sea separates
        the mainland and the island;
                How could I paint a picture

the tone of the lone wrestles with itself
        along undulating waves,
                feet immersed in sharp sand

Herself and myself—The Pacific crashes
        and the threat of that wide open
                beach, the imagined threat

Suddenly all breaks, splits—
        As I drive from one side
                to the other, a childhood drenched

"Now these are the generations of…"
        To reduce the impact,
                I curl my body forward

This passage backward marked
        a meridian, nothing, nobody
                would be the same after

Her body, my body,
        succulents that encompass the
                conflict, the divide,

On the way to that uncharted region,
        the way of contradiction,
                beyond the lighthouse

(if cast in an empty pit,
        a cavity with no water, remember the
                tears buried in past centuries—Now!)

That place, shelter of my imagination,
        out of reach, made of stones
                the size of my stomach

For no apparent reason will a
        child die in its first years—
                a narrow elided fishing line

The anonymous pass from view
        (Would that be too hard to take?)
                no light, and rapture thaws the body

and that changes everything
        the final state, this prolongation
                of vocal sounds

AIR

*The words (she was looking out
the window) sounded as if they
were floating like flowers*

And   she   vanished
into   thin   air

a melody in strophic form

The cold is fierce, the wind, the space available, made available for
the child, pierces walls, double windows and numbs light.

The space available, made available, or unavailable, retracts;
a refuge withdrawn. Her air thins—her breath measured out.

"I cautious, scanned my little life—"

VAPOR   CANNOT   PAINT   A   PICTURE   CAN

I wondered if the heavens were
                        developing large gaps like holes in the ozone.

In the late 20th century, the piercing question is, how much are we willing to exchange for our share of space in the nebula?

In the late 20th century, phantoms in the guise of stellar wind show her a faint tendency towards nothing. She is fissionable.

"Beware lest you lose the substance by grasping at shadows"

    A   SWEET   FIRMAMENT   CHILD   A   SWEET

The aria began as a secret where I
                        was blamed for the part I played in the drama

The presence of seduction confuses the currents, breaks forth in the atmosphere and affects everyone. The keeper of the prison is a wind.

The atmosphere affects everyone and she wonders if there will be enough room for her thoughts to envelop a locality.

Words float on the page, sometimes a phrase, a line or a whole sentence

I   LANDED   IN   A   SOLITUDE   IN

Why is it so difficult for me to find
                                  comfort in a volatile stream?

A genesis lasts a long time and is interpreted each according to the individual's dream. If short of breath listen to gray-hairs before they fall in the grave.

According to the dream she took too much space and had to retreat in the chill currents of the narrow. This influence surrounds her.

"To give some form to the chaos inside me"

DENSE   DAY   DISSEMINATED

For now I see through a glass
              darkly, before being painted over in layers of white

If famine follows it shall be very grievous. A point on the compass. What came to pass caused a complete retreat of her memories into the past.

If famine follows it shall be a blow to the whole mass surrounding the earth, not just one child. Gas evaporates, but leaves a residue.

"The house we were born in is engraved within us"

SHARE   A   BRISK   BREAD

Attachment to crumbs
                        of information, that know only a part

Thinking of elements as well defined personalities is perhaps a mistake; it does not take in boundlessness and emptiness.

A mistake not to think of nothing as not, then we need pneumatic devices to solidify abstractions, and it builds knots.

"Complete collapse. Lack of self-confidence. Aversion. Panic."

    I   COULDN'T   I   ANYTHING   I

That hunger for the absolute must be crushed
                and this grasping at the earth like a buoy in the ether

Whose blood is required so that we can fly over oceans? Refresh your memory. She made herself strange, putting on airs, and lost in brooding.

Whose blood is required? Her memories seek disclosure—confession. Distress found her and she let it come.

"Every word born of an inner necessity"

A   DOUBLE   COULD   TRAVEL   A

It is difficult for us to understand
                each other when we speak through interpreters

THE SPHERE

This is the region of those who hide,
who live buried in a harrowed landscape.

This is the terrain of those who disappear,
for whatever reason, who vanish, melt away.

This is the cenotaph, the crack in the tenor of certain
words, where a country eclipses its own people.

This is the domain of those flailing in the wind,
bounding off surfaces, the narrow regions of the apogee.

We start transparent and then the cloud thickens.
All history backs our panes of glass.

At the edge of my own disappearance,
in the wake of elements that shaped my body,

I turned and noted the treasure that was left
behind in my sacks. I was shy at first,

a mere sliver of the little girl I had been,
afraid the compass would steer me in the wrong,

of exceeding the limits of what was appropriate,
for a "woman" I mean. What I remembered was

the imprecision of this inner life, and my efforts
left me murmuring. How many years were swallowed?

"It is difficult to sing in face of the other."
What was audible? What could be distinguished?

Off the coast, cloaked in a reverie, anchored
in brine, on this almost island, jutting out

My hand reached toward a word, a phrase—
a fragment in this auditorium of noise

where landing on the shoal was obscured
by the repetitive pronouncement that the propertied

were persons of more definite space,
of wide influence, not sediments disturbed.

The pillar I had become disintegrated,
the inconsolable features uncertain of having been,

a variegated landscape, that terrain engraved
by my former state, the path of my past.

A sapling bows its head, soaked by wind.
I shake all over. A leaf hardly formed,

clinging to the groove on this branch,
the weight of it spread out upon her back.

I carry it, these cracks. Her wales. Her burdens.
I washed my flesh and refrained from exposing

the cloud which severed my mind from my body,
(rooted by a law rather than a choice to stand upright).

I had forgotten how to breathe, so that each gasp
came in hurried intervals, uttered the indiscernible.

Bending forward, charred,   blown up at the trunk,
a knot sown at the vista of my imagination.

Washed up on shore during high tide,
secreted on that narrow anatomical strip,

a cephalopod's "rage to order the words of the sea";
copulating with rocks, pebbles, and sand in my

hands—I dug deep into the voices of the past
until I reached a calcified internal shell, all

the pushing in the world couldn't get me past that grip.
Turning away from the bow, my legs about to give way,

to kneel on this raft made of sticks and foliage—
Oceans soften boulders through centuries

if you know how to wait, bit by bit, line by line.
A sea traveler's past seen as no one dares to see it.

The dreamer asks that the woman's life be saved.
Those dying went ashore induced to pretend, to fake it,

the way plants are encouraged to grow indoors.
Who was willing to show how they were torn into pieces?

Arcane knowledge projected its commandments,
and the proper pause was expected before being taken.

I was grieved and angry to be sold to the void,
a slave to the opinion of others, a drop of blood in a toilet,

it put me underground when I was longing for birth.
"Being broken. Speaking broken."

My remains would be found elsewhere, in the aftermath
of a small bedchamber with purple pansies on the night table.

All I could do now was determine my own inner responses
and sterics detected something down there, south of my midriff.

In this globular body my intestines pulpy, shriveled,
weak—the pressure from other regions thrust open

a vulnerable unknown zone, a famished thirsty island,
a longing for something greater than myself.

I forgot that what I hoped for, and at the same time dreaded,
was being completely alone with a blank sheet of paper.

But there is none "whose inward being is so strong
that it is not greatly determined by what lies outside of it."

All holy texts are provisional (you do not see her yet)—
stain that which is not possible to distinguish.

What I had learned was fear, to fear my own thoughts,
my own dreams, my own visions, my own ambition—

the child I had been eclipsed by ideas and beliefs
so solid, so grounded that I became a somber shade

of what I had been, a weary, lusterless eye
sojourning in a foreign land threshed with guts.

My prayers had vanished with the lust
for fame—a storm at the center of the sphere—

and I became a globule of self-restraint
no longer astonished or agitated by the vitality of color.

Extinction happens only to a rare species—
a fade out on the Scribe.

The

Perforated

Map

In us an impulse tests
the unknown

                                        But it is not an end in itself

THE WAIT;

for Homer's Penelope

"Sing in me, Muse, and through me tell the story"

in her room alone

                                      HER INNERMOST

Scrape.   Scratch.   Split.   Jab.
Narrow space prepared for memory.

Yes.   Heavy.   Still.   Yes.   Thick.   Yes.
Why am I pushed to destroy this evening what I made

with my own hands?   "A tendency toward Isolation"?
stitch   prepare   reveal   words   grip   split

Memory can be disputed, bears a distaff.
Marks made in a desperate attempt to find my own.

she almost never shows herself

                                    SUS PEN DED

Unraveling by night   Icy light towers   carried within
I had been led astray to such a point that I was no longer

conscious of what had been done so profoundly.
one   container   scatter   mute   shade

I cannot endure the weight of eternity
in high heels and fishnet stockings

carrying bags of groceries and children.
How can I hope to please a suitor?

her nights and days are wearied out
with grieving

SUP PRESS

Les Pleurs a river through the city—
the source gagged, shut away, hidden.

Swallow   Gulp   enter   Cries   Come
Trepidation a kind of map.   Traces.

All the cooking and then throwing out the dirt.
Meanwhile, a caesura.   Do not erase.

No sword is needed. No need to codify, classify.
I am not waiting for somebody else.

she is in a quandary

                                HESITATES

Spin.   Scraped.   Bit.   Crossed.   Cloaked.
Entangled in a large web, pushed and jostled. Flung.

The orbit of that lineage delayed the dream.
The whole left side of my body aching to…

The mouth must be opened, stretched wide
to make a sound in American, then closed for "th"

hold   back   the   void
there is "always another and another and…"

for not to everyone will the gods appear

                              TICIP

Travelers are fragile so we build up our nails,
clocks hook into our hearts which wall us in

lit   lamp   roam   ride   stitch   sense
I did not listen to the news nor read the papers.

I sat alone. Why make us like that, with a big
hole in the middle? Room for stones?

mocking echo
                                          mocking echo

her shinning veil across her cheeks

                              HOVERS

The enigma   led home   a pair of large hands
feeling   for a face,   the curves   hurled forth

Twenty years gone and a fractured body is drawn
back to the frozen portals of the island.

My hairpins fall out one after the other as
I open the shutters which give sound to windows.

STITCH   RAVAGE   HELD   TERROR   SHAPE
Listen.   A poem is the suitcase of the exile.

she caught back the swift words upon her tongue
then softly she withdrew

                                      BURD

Caught in the act   the long threads pulled out
The pillars of our mouth   prepare the story

when singing: I… I… I… I…
identified with… a substitute? a double? a body?

fine wool disintegrates in dark dwellings—
words rise which name and rename

Bathed in crimson clouds   the trail begins
What is at stake here? What is essential?

she returns alone and lays again on her forsaken
bed—sodden how often with weeping

                              THE ORDEAL

Ask a question. Ask a savage question. Dare to ask it.
Alone. Rise through it. Not quickly. Ask it. Again.

Not so quickly as to take all the pleasure out of it.
What dream? What fantasy? What story? What sign?

Ask me who I was before the clock began ticking.
Don't anticipate the answer, be patient, hear me.

I learned to keep my head in hardship.
Let this new trial come. Ask me.

on an island
gentle lady
meanwhile
the reminded

                    INTERIM

I had no preview of what would happen next, no encapsulating review. After my third year the earth was inside.

"They say when one is about to die the fingers curl
to a close"   Clenched fist.

Again, why am I pushed to destroy this evening
what I had created with my own hands?

What is within…   What must be read…
"each step an ache"   toward the turning…

they go in foreign guise, the gods do, looking
like strangers, turning up in towns and
settlements to keep an eye…

                              THE SORROW

While other things were going on around the world
my images opened a space which I had closed before

the flood. Since you asked… How long ago was it?
Seems like centuries. I unlaced my notes by torchlight.

If I let in what I make every day I would be overwhelmed.
drive   gales   white   wheels   water

I couldn't pronounce that word. A question of enunciation.
Language   my   mask

let her tell the tale again for our own ears

                                                  FFLICTION

A.
Laughter seized me.

Convulsive.   Rip.
Words hide as much as they reveal.

I was called "the wise." The wise!
The label fit in a place I could not touch.

They would forget me then in this rarefied atmosphere.
My tongue large. Je ne peut pas. Je ne peut pas. Chained.

may death come all of a sudden; may death
relieve us as clean as that

        SEACURSE

"Everyone who has seen, sees farther.
                             even farther than allowed."

How to PATIENCE how to SPEAK how to
A   child   born   out   of   the   ear.   Écoute.

Listen,   interpret me this dream:
I am on a panel with Susan Howe and Tennyson…

Night comes, the wind dies down, space thickens,
and I in my skin hopping around. Where is the answer?

of mortal creature, all that breathe and more, earth
bears none frailer than mankind

                              WAIT

The heartache will pass.
Behind the curtain nothing as frightening as that.

I was a child then, well, I am not now.
I just wanted everything in my mouth.

I bit off needle and thread.
No one mentions the tapestry I created.

The clock will forget my labors. Born.
Halt.   Continue.   Halt.   Continue.

WEAVE STOP WEAVE GO WEAVE STOP WEAVE GO

the scar

the scarred thigh

she knew the grooves at once

                                      AD MISSION

My legacy is revealed by the mark on my body.
Bit. Pounded. Coaxed. Cradled. Ripped. Aroused.

A few simple words that I could twist made it past
the nucleus and logged themselves permanently.

I could not know myself until now——not until I knew
my own body with my hands. Bring out what is within.

I made the mistake of fighting with my parts.
Bring out what is within.   O the bliss of petals.

who sends an arrow

THE ARENA

Forgetting is the most complicated of locks,
but it is only a lock, one of subtle ways.

In one motion I slid my hand down and plucked the cord
so taut that vibrating it hummed and sang a swallows note.

Pulled off into a handkerchief are the lists,
drawings,   notes,   quotes,   and   comments.

Decipher the marks of time (America's are written on buses)
the subtlest scratch is present and does perform.

so now in turn each woman thrust her head into a noose
and swung, yanked high in the air to perish there
most piteously

DESIRCROSS

How could I ever get past this point? A hammer oscillates.
They were not "wise" so were strung up on photographs?

I could not separate myself from them. My own murder.
The back and forth motion made me nauseous.

I cannot stand apart from my own kind.
I too open like a ring to bleed.

CA RESS
KISS

for a long time she sat deathly still and waited

                                        AH…

I am stunned. I cannot speak. I cannot keep my eyes open.
There.   There.   There's the sign.   The secret.

I remember they all do wait.   Yes.   Wait.   Yes.
"They" meaning other women. My knees grew weak.

I armed myself long ago against the frauds and impostors
who might come, and then I walked right in all the same.

Caught like the small animal that was my life
the words and phrases left unfinished.

but here and now, what sign could be so clear as
this of her own bed

                                        WET

Rhymes and rhythms open in the arms of another.
Awaiting the downfall of the mask…

In that bed where a touch held steadfast to my skin
eyelashes graze mountains while seas open into a cavern.

Ripe.
Rumble.

be my

witness

she told of what hard blows she had dealt out to
others and what blows she had taken

                                        SEEKlust

I take him inside when he comes without warning.
I ask him again, what is essential?

I discover my own violence and a torrent as I
lower unto him the excitement I had wound myself in.

Let me speak so that you can enter
so that we can come together.

They said I was "valiant" "wife" "true" "faithful"
When you feel nice all over its hard to remember others.

HOT. STILL. YES.
When he came back after twenty years I was no longer eleven.

NOTES

WALE; or The Corse

"Open your lips; don't open them simply. I don't open them simply." Luce Irigaray, *This Sex Which is Not One*, translated by Catherine Porter.

"Whole world seems against me if I could just explain. Man I love has left me because I called…" Ma Rainey.

"Her cry silences whole vocabularies of names for things." Susan Howe, *The Europe of Trusts*.

"I am tormented with an everlasting itch for things remote." Herman Melville, *Moby-Dick*.

"Meditation and water are wedded forever." Melville, *Moby-Dick*.

"The whale cannot digest me." H.D., *Trilogy*, from *The Collected Poems*.

Unknowne Land

"Nothing will be retained from them, which they have imagined to do." *The Bible*. "Genesis," 11:6 (All references to *The Bible* are taken from the King James Version).

"Does not our lives consist of the four elements?—Faith, so they say, but I think it rather consists of eating and drinking." William Shakespeare, *Twelfth Night*.

"the noises in the darkness of the night… the groans of the wounded… filled with their cries." Leo N. Tolstoy, *War and Peace*, translated by Rosemary Edmonds.

"An altar of stone" *The Bible*, "Exodus," 20:25.

"Brought forth into this wilderness." *The Bible*, "Exodus," 16:3.

"An alien in a strange land." *The Bible*, "Exodus," 18:3.

"broken me asunder… taken me by the neck and shaken me to pieces" *The Bible.* "Job," 12:16.

"…*all that powers weeping savagely in and inevitably withdrawing, hypnotized, and the two senses of that vastness and this tininess…*" Virginia Woolf, *To the Lighthouse.*

"A word will never be able to comprehend the voice that utters it." Thomas Merton, *New Seeds of Contemplation.*

"I take it slow." Lorine Niedecker, *From This Condensery; Complete Works.*

"What if then *is* now?" Susan Howe, "Encloser." *The Politics of Poetic Form*, ed. Charles Bernstein.

"and the sudden silent trout all lit up, hanging, trembling" Virginia Woolf, *To the Lighthouse.*

"Now these are the generations of…" *The Bible,* "Genesis," 36:1.

The words (she was looking out the window) sounded as if they were floating like flowers. Virginia Woolf, *To the Lighthouse.*

"I cautious, scanned my little life—" Emily Dickinson, *The Complete Poems*, #178.

"Beware lest you lose the substance by grasping at shadows." Aesop.

"To give some form to the chaos inside me." Etty Hillesum, *An Interrupted Life*, translated by Arnold J. Pomerans.

"it shall be very grievous." *The Bible.* "Genesis," 41:31

"The house we were born in [has] engraved within us…" Gaston Bachelard, *The Poetics of Space*, translated by Maria Jolas.

"Complete collapse. Lack of self-confidence. Aversion. Panic." Etty Hillesum, *An Interrupted Life*, translated by Arnold J. Pomerans.

"Every word born of an inner necessity." Etty Hillesum, *An Interrupted Life*, translated by Arnold J. Pomerans.

We start transparent and then the cloud thickens. All history backs our panes of glass. Virginia Woolf, *Jacob's Room.*

"rage to order the words of the sea." Wallace Stevens, *The Collected Poems*.

"Being broken. Speaking broken." Theresa Hak Kyung Cha, *Dictée*.

"whose inward being is so strong that it is not greatly determined by what lies outside of it." George Eliot, *Middlemarch*.

THE WAIT; for Homer's Penelope

This poem utilizes language from *The Odyssey* by Homer, translated by Robert Fitzgerald.

Lightning Source UK Ltd.
Milton Keynes UK
UKHW010702221020
372035UK00001B/31